W9-BTI-091

Be A
Pet Expert

BE A DOG EXPERT

By Gemma Barder

CRABTREE
PUBLISHING COMPANY
WWW.CRABTREEBOOKS.COM

BE A DOG EXPERT

Dogs are great! They are the world's most popular pet and it's easy to see why. Dogs are loving and loyal, but they need a lot of care and attention. In this book you'll learn everything you need to know about looking after your dog, setting up the perfect home for it, and the best way to keep your furry friend happy and healthy. You'll also find out how dogs became such ideal companions, and learn some pretty incredible **canine** facts along the way.

CRABTREE
PUBLISHING COMPANY
WWW.CRABTREEBOOKS.COM

Published in Canada
Crabtree Publishing
616 Welland Avenue
St. Catharines, ON
L2M 5V6

Published in the United States
Crabtree Publishing
347 Fifth Ave,
Suite 1402-145
New York, NY 10016

Published in 2021 by CRABTREE PUBLISHING COMPANY.

First published in 2019 by Wayland
Copyright © Hodder and Stoughton, 2019

Author: Gemma Barder

Editorial director: Kathy Middleton

Editors: Dynamo Limited, Robin Johnson

Cover and interior design: Dynamo Limited

Proofreader: Melissa Boyce

**Production coordinator
& Prepress technician:** Samara Parent

Print coordinator: Katherine Berti

Printed in the U.S.A./072020/CG20200429

Photographs
(l - left, r - right, tl - top left, tr - top right, cr - center right, bl - bottom left)

All images courtesy of Getty Images iStock except:
Kuznetsov Alexey/Shutterstock: front cover and title page l; Jagodka/Shutterstock: front cover and title page r; Eric Isselee/Shutterstock: 4bl, 22tl; Blanka Berankova/Shutterstock: 7 tl, ; Westend61 GmbH/Alamy 7 cr; Golden Pixels LLC/Shutterstock: 12tr; Mariia Boiko/Shutterstock: 28

Pictorial Press Ltd/Alamy: 21c; Tierfotoagentur/Alamy: 23tr

Every attempt has been made to clear copyright. Should there be any inadvertent omission, please apply to the publisher for rectification.

Library and Archives Canada Cataloguing in Publication

Title: Be a dog expert / by Gemma Barder.
Other titles: Dogs
Names: Barder, Gemma, author.
Description: Series statement: Be a pet expert |
  Previously published under title: Dogs. | Includes index.
Identifiers: Canadiana (print) 20200222414 |
  Canadiana (ebook) 20200222422 |
  ISBN 9780778780168 (hardcover) |
  ISBN 9780778780441 (softcover) |
  ISBN 9781427125583 (HTML)
Subjects: LCSH: Dogs—Juvenile literature. |
  LCSH: Dog breeds—Juvenile literature.
Classification: LCC SF426.5 .B37 2021 | DDC j636.7/0887—dc23

Library of Congress Cataloging-in-Publication Data

Names: Barder, Gemma, author.
Title: Be a dog expert / by Gemma Barder.
Description: New York : Crabtree Publishing Company, 2021. |
  Series: Be a pet expert | Includes index.
Identifiers: LCCN 2020015996 (print) | LCCN 2020015997 (ebook) |
  ISBN 9780778780168 (hardcover) |
  ISBN 9780778780441 (paperback) |
  ISBN 9781427125583 (ebook)
Subjects: LCSH: Dogs--Juvenile literature.
Classification: LCC SF426.5 .B365 2021 (print) | LCC SF426.5 (ebook) |
  DDC 636.7--dc23
LC record available at https://lccn.loc.gov/2020015996
LC ebook record available at https://lccn.loc.gov/2020015997

CONTENTS

PUPPIES

THE CANINE
CODE

DOGGY
DATA

THE BEST
BED

DOGS, DOGS, DOGS!

Although there are a dizzying number of dog **breeds**, they are divided into seven groups according to their relationship with humans over time.

TERRIER GROUP

There are many different terrier breeds and they are all confident, energetic, highly intelligent dogs, which makes them great family pets. Their name comes from the Latin word *terra*, which means "earth," because terriers were originally used to hunt small burrowing **prey** such as rabbits, rats, and mice.

MINIATURE SCHNAUZER

This neat little dog is a mix of a standard schnauzer, poodle, and affenpinscher.

AIREDALE

These brave little dogs were the first police dogs in the United Kingdom and worked with British soldiers in World War I (1914–1918).

JACK RUSSELL

This breed gets its name from the Reverend John Russell, who first bred them.

WORKING GROUP

A working dog is any breed that was traditionally raised to perform a job. This could include pulling a sled, guarding property, or rescuing people.

GREAT DANE

These gentle giants are one of the tallest dog breeds in the world.

SIBERIAN HUSKY

These dogs have double layers of fur that keep them warm in cold weather.

SAINT BERNARD

This classic rescue dog is named after a dangerous spot in the Swiss Alps called the Great Saint Bernard Pass.

TOY GROUP

Toy dogs evolved from lapdog breeds (dogs that fit nicely into the lap to be petted and cuddled) as well as common breeds that have been bred to be smaller, such as the miniature poodle.

SHIH TZU

This adorable breed comes from Tibet and dates back at least 1,000 years.

CHIHUAHUA

This tiny pup is the smallest dog breed in the world.

MALTESE

This well-mannered breed is thought to be the oldest European toy dog breed.

THE OTHER DOG GROUPS ARE:

SPORTING GROUP: These dogs were bred to work with hunters to find and pick up prey. Golden retrievers, cocker spaniels, and Irish setters are all sporting dogs.

HERDING GROUP: These dogs were bred to help look after, **herd**, or guard livestock such as cows and sheep. Border collies, corgis, and Old English sheepdogs are in the herding group.

NON-SPORTING GROUP: This group consists of dogs that do not fit into other groups. They vary in size, appearance, and personality. Non-sporting dogs include bulldogs, dalmatians, and poodles.

HOUND GROUP

Like terriers, hounds are hunting dogs. They have an incredible sense of smell, are strong and capable, and often have long, droopy ears. This group also contains some of the oldest-known dog breeds still around today.

DACHSHUND

This breed's long, flexible body makes it perfect for wriggling into burrows after small animals!

WHIPPET

These friendly dogs are very quiet, so they might not make the best guard dogs! Some whippets don't bark at all.

BASSET HOUND

This dog's floppy ears aren't just for show! They flap smells up from the ground, making this breed a super-sniffing tracker.

UNCOMMON DOGS

Dogs are everywhere, right? But some breeds are so rare, there are only a few hundred animals left. Take a look at some of these special dogs.

Otterhounds have been around since the 1600s!

OTTERHOUND

This breed comes from England and has a playful personality. Otterhounds were originally bred to hunt but are now mainly show dogs and family pets. Despite their sweet nature, there are only 600 otterhounds in the world.

Otterhounds have webbed feet, which makes them great swimmers!

 # NEW GUINEA SINGING DOG

This little dog really lives up to its name. The New Guinea singing dog has a unique way of howling that is much more musical than other dogs. Although few of these dogs live as pets, some scientists believe there could be many more in the wild.

TELOMIAN

These dogs were first bred in the Malaysian jungle in Southeast Asia, and they are still the only breed of Malaysian dog found outside the country. Telomians were originally kept to get rid of mice and rats (like cats do) but they are now mainly family pets. Although they don't look that different from other dogs, they developed amazing climbing skills because their original owners lived in jungle houses on stilts!

FACT FILE

The most endangered breeds in the world are actually wild dogs.

■ The Ethiopian wolf is found in the highlands of Ethiopia in Africa. Fewer than 500 are alive today.

■ The Mexican gray wolf is half the size of its North American cousin. Scientists believe there are fewer than 200 of them in the wild.

■ Darwin's fox is actually a small wolf the same size as an average cat. It is almost extinct in the wild.

DID YOU KNOW?

Dogs are part of a large family called Canidae, which also includes wolves, foxes, coyotes, and jackals.

DOGGY LANGUAGE

Dogs are great at communicating with their human buddies. Here is everything you need to know to understand what your pal is trying to tell you!

FACT FILE

When you meet a new dog, there are a few things you should do to make a great first impression:

■ Ask the owner's permission before you say hello. Some dogs can be shy or nervous.

■ Let the dog sniff your hand. (Sniffing in the doggy world is like shaking hands in the world of humans.)

■ Speak softly and calmly to the dog.

TAIL

Dogs **wag** their tails when they are in a happy and playful mood. Your pup will usually wag its tail when it first sees you or if you are playing together. Dogs put their tails between their legs when they are scared, sad, or even if they feel guilty about stealing food off the kitchen table!

BELLY

Your dog will show its belly when it wants to make friends with other dogs—or when it wants a tummy rub from you!

8

EARS

The position of a dog's ears can tell you a lot about how the dog is feeling. If their ears are perked up, your dog is relaxed and happy. If they are slightly forward, your dog is alert. When the ears are back, your dog is unhappy or **anxious**, and when they are flattened down, that means your dog is afraid.

NOSE

A dry nose could be a sign that your dog is sick. It could also mean that your dog needs a drink or has just woken up from a nap.

TEETH

Dogs show their teeth when they are angry or upset. This could be because they are afraid of another dog or are angry at being in pain. Pet dogs don't usually show their teeth, so if they do, something is probably wrong. Give your dog space to calm down.

LEGS

A dog that is scared or anxious will lower its front legs so it is crouching down, or it might have one paw in the air preparing to run if it needs to. Happy dogs will have their legs straight or slightly bent, ready to play!

PUPPIES

These adorable little bundles need a lot of love and attention because they are no longer with their mothers. Now it's up to you to help your **puppy** develop and grow!

PICKING A PUPPY

Picking the right puppy for your home is very important. Talk to your family about what type of dog would suit you best. Bigger dogs need more room and a big yard to play in, while long-haired breeds need plenty of brushing.

All puppies are cute when they are little, but they grow up fast!

BRINGING IT HOME

Puppies can be quite nervous when they are taken to their new homes. Make sure you have a comfy dog **carrier** to put your puppy in and a blanket to keep it warm. If the journey home is long, make sure you have plenty of water and food for it too.

Give your new puppy plenty of love and play with it every day to welcome it into your family.

FACT FILE

In the first few months:

■ Find a vet and get your PUPPY used to visiting them. The vet will give your PUPPY vaccinations and medicine it needs to stay healthy.

■ Train your PUPPY to pee and poop outside.

■ Ask your vet when your PUPPY will be ready to go outside. Then take your PUPPY for short walks to get it used to other dogs.

DID YOU KNOW?
In some countries, there are laws that you must have your new puppy microchipped. The tiny microchip is placed painlessly inside your puppy's neck and has all your contact information on it.

WELCOME HOME
While your new puppy settles into your home, remember to keep things calm and quiet. Your pup will be learning all about its new environment—and all about you too!

9 weeks

5-6 pups

Female dogs are pregnant for nine weeks.

An average litter has five to six puppies.

CANINE CARE

It goes without saying that you want your dog to be the happiest it can be. Find out the best ways to care for your furry friend.

NEW BEST FRIEND

Dogs are social animals. In the wild, they live in packs. They can be unhappy if they are left alone, so spend plenty of time with your dog. You could play in the yard, brush your dog's fur, or just tell it about your day!

KEEPING CLEAN

A well-groomed dog is a happy dog. Grooming means making sure your dog is brushed and clean. Different breeds need different amounts of grooming, so make sure you know what's right for your pet.

WALK ON!

One of the most important parts of looking after a dog is exercise. Dogs need to be walked at least once a day, and some breeds need more exercise than others. Make sure you have a good leash, some dog treats, and pet waste bags for picking up poop.

DID YOU KNOW?

Clipping a dog's nails is tricky and should be done by a vet. You can also take your dog to a grooming parlor (a doggy hairdresser) to get its fur and nails trimmed.

A dog needs two bowls— one for a constant supply of fresh water and another for its daily meals.

FLEAS AND WORMS

Although it's not very nice to think about, fleas and worms are a common problem for dogs. The best way to help your pet is to give it monthly treatments to prevent it from getting fleas and worms. Your vet can tell you the best type of treatment for your dog.

2 months **3 weeks**

Dogs need their claws trimmed every two months. Don't bathe your dog more than once every three weeks because that could irritate its skin.

FACT FILE

TRAINING DAY!

It's a good idea to teach your dog these basic commands:

SIT

This is important when you are waiting to cross the road on walks.

STAY

Use this command when you don't want your dog to follow you.

COME

This command is important for getting your dog to come back to you when it is off its leash.

FETCH

This is a fun throw-and-bring-back game to keep your dog happy and fit.

Give your dog a lot of praise and a little treat when it does something right!

THE CANINE CODE

There are a lot of rules to follow when you own a dog, and it can get pretty confusing! Follow these simple guidelines to become the perfect dog owner.

DO:

Introduce your dog to other dogs to get them used to being around other animals.

Give your dog a short name—one or two syllables is best. And avoid names that sound like commands!

Pick up your dog's poop using a biodegradable bag, put it in the garbage, and wash your hands afterward.

Give your pup plenty of toys to play with. Dogs like to be kept active.

Check your dog's paws for small stones after it's been on a long walk.

Treat your dog like one of the family. Dogs love to be part of a pack!

DON'T:

 ✗

Don't pull a dog's tail. It will hurt and confuse them.

 ✗

Don't leave your dog's water bowl empty or dirty. Dogs need fresh water to keep them healthy.

 ✗

Don't force your dog to play with dogs it isn't used to.

 ✗

Don't give your dog chocolate. Chocolate can be poisonous to dogs.

 ✗

Don't leave your dog alone for long periods of time.

 ✗

Don't let your dog off its leash unless you are in a large field or park where this is allowed.

✓ FOOD FOR DOGS ✗

apples	dry dog food	avocado	grapes
cheese	wet dog food	chocolate	nuts
cooked fish	yogurt	dried fruit	onions

THE BEST BED

When you love your pet, you want to give it the best home possible. Find out how to make a safe and cozy home for your dog.

SAFE AND SOUND

Making your house safe for a dog is a bit like babyproofing. Look around the rooms your dog will call home to spot any dangers, such as wires it might chew on, blinds it could get tangled in, or cleaning products it could mistake for treats or toys.

BEDTIME

A dog's bed is very important to it. It's not just the snuggle factor you need to think about, but where you put the bed too. Make sure the bed is in a place where your dog can watch family life go by and feel like it is part of the action.

THE GREAT OUTDOORS

Your dog should spend a lot of time in the yard, so you will need to make it a fun and safe place. Check that there are no holes in the fence and that the gate is secure. Keep an eye out for any dog poop and clean it up right away.

KEEP IT CLEAN

Keeping your dog's home clean and tidy is an important way to keep your pet healthy. Wash your dog's food bowl after every meal and its bedding once a week.

FACT FILE

Here are some dog beds to choose from:

NEST
This dog bed has a round, padded middle with soft edges that form a cozy nest. It is perfect for small to medium-sized dogs.

CAVE
These beds have little hoods and are great for dogs that feel the cold, such as hairless breeds.

MATTRESS
This dog bed looks just like a mattress for people! It is perfect for large dogs that like to spread out.

DID YOU KNOW?
Dogs love toys! Toys help keep dogs occupied and relaxed, and stop them from chewing on other things—like the furniture!

WALKING THROUGH TIME

Dogs have been our best buddies for a very long time. Learn how these four-legged friends have traveled through history with us.

STATUS SYMBOL

As thousands of years passed, dogs became seen as symbols of wealth and power. Ancient Egyptian rulers had dogs as companions, and dogs were highly valued as part of the family.

38,000 B.C.E.   **3100 B.C.E.**   **1200s–1600s**

HUNGRY LIKE THE WOLF

The first **domesticated** canines are thought to be wolves that followed human tribes around looking for scraps of food. Some scientists believe this could have started as early as 40,000 years ago! Over time, wolves started traveling with the tribes and humans began training them.

PAMPERED PETS

Many **noble** families had pet dogs, which is why dogs often pop up in portraits of important people. Noblewomen preferred smaller dogs they could rest on their laps, while noblemen liked powerful hunting dogs.

DID YOU KNOW?

In 1789, a Newfoundland dog saved a man from drowning off the coast of Portsmouth, United Kingdom. The man was so thankful, he bought the dog, named him Friend, and created a coat of arms just for him!

The basenji is one of the oldest dog breeds in the world. People say it resembles the dogs kept by ancient Egyptian rulers.

A HELPING PAW

In the 1950s, a study done by a doctor named Boris M. Levinson showed how dogs could be used in therapy sessions. He found that people were more relaxed and able to talk when a dog was there to make them feel safe and happy.

1800s

1950s

2000s

VICTORIAN LOVE

By the Victorian era, most middle-class homes had dogs. Some people began to train their pets to compete in dog shows. In 1891, Queen Victoria (1819–1901) entered six Pomeranians in an international dog show in the United Kingdom.

DOGS TODAY

Dogs are still the most popular pets in the world (followed closely by cats). They have continued to serve and help humans in many different ways, including rescuing people, herding cattle, guiding people who are blind, working with the police, being loving companions, and so much more!

FAMOUS FURRY FRIENDS

Dogs have such great personalities, it's no wonder some become famous! Find out the fascinating stories behind some of the most well-known pooches.

TOTO

Toto is the scrappy little pup who joins Dorothy on her adventures in *The Wizard of Oz*. He has appeared in books, movies, and television series based on the world of Oz. He even has a book written from his point of view called *Toto: the Dog-Gone Amazing Story of The Wizard of Oz*.

LASSIE

Some say the helpful dog named Lassie first appeared as a character in a British short story. Others believe she was based on a real dog that saved a sailor's life in World War I. However, Lassie became known all over the world thanks to the 1943 movie *Lassie Come Home* and the TV shows that followed.

DID YOU KNOW?
The first dog to play Lassie was actually a male dog named Pal! He played the part of the famous female dog for 11 years.

CORGIS

Queen Elizabeth II has had more than 30 corgis during her reign. She was first given a Welsh corgi puppy on her eighteenth birthday and then went on to raise them for many years. Her last corgi was named Willow and was the fourteenth generation of the queen's first pup.

SCOOBY-DOO!

Scooby is a Great Dane who helps his friends solve spooky mysteries—and always makes time to eat Scooby Snacks with his best friend Shaggy. The first Scooby-Doo cartoon was shown in 1969 and the dopey dog is still around today. There have been TV shows, movies, and even video games featuring Scooby and the gang.

Lassie was a collie, like this dog.

$10,000

$125

Moose the dog was paid $10,000 per episode to star in the TV series *Frasier*. The little dog who played Toto in *The Wizard of Oz* was paid $125 a week—which was more than most actors got paid in 1939 when the film came out!.

TOP DOGS

Whether they're big, small, brave, or unusual, these dogs have something in common—they are all record breakers!

TALL AND SHORT

The tallest dog ever was Zeus, a Great Dane like this one. He measured a massive 44 inches (111 cm) tall. On the other hand, Milly the Chihuahua is the smallest dog at just 3.8 inches (9.65 cm) tall!

This little Chihuahua is much bigger than Milly!

SPACE DOG

Laika was a very special dog. In 1957, she became the first animal to orbit Earth. What the space scientists learned from her trip helped make it possible for humans to travel safely in space.

89.7 million   **5.9 million**

There are 89.7 million pet dogs in the United States.

There are 5.9 million pet dogs in Canada.

Australian cattle dogs can live for a very long time!

OLDEST DOG

In 1939, a hard-working Australian cattle dog named Bluey became the oldest dog ever when he lived to the age of 29 years and 5 months. The average life span of a dog is between 10 and 13 years, although some smaller breeds can live longer.

LONGEST TONGUE

Mochi the Saint Bernard is the lucky owner of the longest dog tongue in the world. His tongue measures 7.3 inches (18.58 cm) and is so big it usually hangs out of his mouth. Despite Mochi's strange claim to fame, his owners think he is the cutest dog on the block.

Many Saint Bernards have long tongues!

DOGGY DATA

If you think you know everything about dogs, be prepared to be amazed. Memorize these five facts to impress your friends.

1 CANINE NOSES ARE UNIQUE

The print a dog's nose makes is one of a kind, just like a human fingerprint.

2 WILD AT HEART

Dogs curl up to sleep because they were once wild animals like wolves. Wolves curl up to keep warm and protect their bodies from **predators**.

3 DALMATIANS DON'T ALWAYS HAVE SPOTS

When Dalmatians are born they are almost always pure white. Their spots develop as they grow.

4 GREYHOUNDS ARE SUPER SPEEDY

They are the fastest breed of dog and can run at speeds of more than 45 miles per hour (72 kph).

5 LABRADORS ARE SO PUP-ULAR!

In fact, Labrador retrievers are the most popular breed of dog in the world. They make good pets for families with a lot of energy and space to grow.

YOUR DREAM DOG

Can you match your personality to your dream dog? Answer the questions and follow the arrows to find out!

WHAT ARE WEEKENDS FOR?

Relaxing

DO YOU LIKE READING?

Yes

Sometimes

I'm a bit shy

Activities

DO YOU LIKE MAKING NEW FRIENDS?

I love it!

No

ARE YOU ON A SPORTS TEAM OR IN A CLUB?

Yes

WHAT'S BETTER— SPOTS OR STRIPES?

Stripes

Spots

DO YOU LIKE LONG WALKS IN THE COUNTRY?

Yes

Sometimes

No

ARE PARTIES ALL ABOUT DANCING?

Yes

AT SCHOOL DO YOU PREFER PHYS ED OR DRAMA CLASS?

Drama

Phys Ed

Maybe

DO YOU LIKE GOING FOR A RUN?

Yes

TIBETAN TERRIER
Sit down, relax, and take a deep breath. That's your guide to life! Like Tibetan terriers, you're a super easygoing person who loves long walks as much as curling up by the fire with a good book.

CHIHUAHUA
Ooh, look! A group of people! There must be something fun going on over there! Just like Chihuahuas, you love being part of the action and making new friends.

DALMATIAN
If you can sit down long enough to read this you'll realize that you and Dalmatians just love being active and having fun. You're also naturally stylish. Spots are so in!

QUIZ!

Now let's put everything you have learned in this book to the test! It's time to find out if you are a real doggy expert.

1 WHERE DOES THE NAME "TERRIER" COME FROM?

a) the name of the person who started breeding them
b) the Latin name for "earth" because they were bred to dig for prey
c) the word "terror" because they can be quite fierce

2 WHAT SHOULD YOU DO WHEN YOU SEE A DOG YOU DON'T KNOW?

a) ask the owner if you can pet their dog
b) run over and pet its back
c) throw it a ball

3 HOW LONG ARE FEMALE DOGS PREGNANT FOR?

a) four weeks
b) nine weeks
c) twenty weeks

4 HOW OFTEN SHOULD YOU WALK YOUR DOG?

a) at least once a day
b) once a week
c) once every two weeks

The answers can be found on page 30.

6 WHAT TYPE OF BED IS PERFECT FOR HAIRLESS DOGS?

a) cave
b) mattress
c) nest

5 WHICH OF THESE FOODS CAN BE POISONOUS TO DOGS?

a) apples
b) yogurt
c) chocolate

7 WHAT TYPE OF DOGS DID QUEEN VICTORIA ENTER INTO A DOG SHOW?

a) Welsh corgis
b) Labrador retrievers
c) Pomeranians

8 WHAT MOVIE FEATURES
TOTO THE DOG?

a) *Cinderella*
b) *The Wizard of Oz*
c) *Mary Poppins*

9 WHAT DOES
A DALMATIAN
LOOK LIKE
WHEN IT'S
BORN?

a) white
b) spotty
c) hairless

10 WHICH OF THESE
DOGS HAS AMAZING
CLIMBING SKILLS?

a) Telomian
b) Saint Bernard
c) Chihuahua

QUIZ ANSWERS

1b 2a 3b 4a 5c 6a 7c 8b 9a 10a

GLOSSARY

anxious
Worried or nervous

biodegradable
Able to be broken down
naturally over time

breed
A group of animals that share
the same characteristics and
physical appearance

canine
A member of the dog family
or anything relating to dogs

carrier
A container big enough to
transport a dog in, usually
made out of plastic, with air
holes and a handle

coat of arms
Special pictures or symbols
that belong to a person,
family, or group and are
shown on a shield

domesticated
Living with humans as pets or
working animals

endangered
At risk of dying out

extinct
Describing a species of animal
or plant that has died out

herd
To gather and move a group
of animals

litter
A group of baby animals born
at the same time to the same
mother

noble
Belonging to the highest social
class

predator
An animal that hunts and eats
other animals

prey
Animals that are hunted and
eaten by other animals

puppy
A young dog

vaccination
A substance injected by needle
into an animal or person to
protect against disease

vet
An animal doctor; short for
veterinarian

wag
To move quickly from side
to side

INDEX